The Flame and the Human Family

The Flame and the Human Family

The Flame and the Human Family

The Flame and the Human Family

The Flame and the Human Family

By Dean Nkulumo Maphenduka
Umlindi WeLangabi Elingcwele
Guardian of the Sacred Flame

Kiye Media Publishing
Loganville, GA 30052

Contact: info@flameofone.org | info@kiyebooks.com

The Flame and the Human Family

© 2025 Dean Nkulumo Maphenduka. All rights reserved.

No part of this publication may be reproduced, stored in a retrieval system, or transmitted in any form or by any means electronic, mechanical, photocopying, recording, or otherwise without the prior written permission of the publisher.

Published by Kiye Media Publishing, Loganville, GA 30052
ISBN: 978-1-7334237-3-1

Printed in the United States of America

The Flame and the Human Family

Contents

Dedication 3
Foreword 4
Author's Note 5
Prologue: Invocation 6
Part 1: The Human Family 7
Chapter One: The Story of Us 9
Chapter Two: What Divides Us, What Unites Us 13
Chapter Three: Race, Roots, and the Rainbow of Creation ... 18
Part II: The Flame Within 23
Chapter Four: Every Soul Has a Spark 25
Chapter 5: Faith Beyond the Fence 30
Chapter 6: Healing from Religion, Returning to God 32
Part III: Wounded World, Sacred Path 36
Chapter 7: The Age of Fear and the Call of Love 37
Chapter 8: Stories from the Firelight 41
Chapter 9: The Way of the Flame (practices, community, call to action) . 49
Epilogue 53
Letter to the Flamebearers 55
Blessing 57
A Prayer for the World 58
A Final Word: 61

The Flame and the Human Family

Dedication

To every soul who has felt alone, divided, or dimmed, may this flame remind you: you are not forgotten, and you were never meant to glow in solitude.

Foreword

In a time when the world feels divided by race, religion, and fear, this book arrives as a sacred offering a path back to our shared light. The Flame and the Human Family reminds us that we are one family under God, and that love, not labels, is what binds us. Dean Nkulumo Maphenduka's message is timeless and timely. You hold not just a book, but a beacon.

The Flame and the Human Family

Author's Note

For decades, I carried this vision quietly, believing its time would come. I wrote this book not to create a new religion, but to return us to the truth beneath all faiths: that we are loved, created in light, and called to love one another as family. If you find yourself within these pages, then it was written for you.

Dean Nkulumo Maphenduka,
Umlindi WeLangabi Elingcwele
Guardian of the Sacred Flame

Prologue: Invocation

Let this flame be the light that wakes us.
The ember in the ash. The hush before the dawn.
May it burn through illusion, melt away fear,
And remind each soul of its belonging.

This is not a doctrine. It is a remembering.
This is not a sermon. It is a rising.
This is not the start of something new,
But the return to what has always been true.

Let those who have been scattered come home.
Let those whose fires dimmed be rekindled.
Let this be the circle we step into,
With grace, with courage, with flame.

Part 1: The Human Family

We are many nations, many tongues, many colors but one humanity. In every village, every city, every continent, there are stories of love, struggle, triumph, and grace. These chapters explore the divine design of human diversity and how race, when honored, can unite rather than divide.

The Flame and the Human Family

Chapter One: The Story of Us

We are not new to this world.
We've been walking it for a very long time barefoot, burdened, beautiful.
Before there were borders or flags, before languages were divided by oceans and war, we were one. One family. One breath. One sacred flame.

And then something happened.
We forgot.

Somewhere along the way, we stopped looking at each other with wonder and started measuring.
We began drawing lines in the dirt between color and country, between belief and name and decided who was better, who was worth more, who could belong, and who could be cast out.

We created stories to make sense of our pain.
Some of those stories became tribes. Some became temples. Some became cages.

The Flame and the Human Family

If you sit quietly beneath the hum of screens, beneath the layers of

noise that modern life piles on, you can still feel the old ache.
It's not just loneliness. It's disconnection.
We ache because we were made to belong to one another, and we've forgotten how.

This book isn't here to sell you a solution.
It's not another program, or platform, or perfect doctrine.
It's an invitation. A remembering.

Because buried beneath the fear and cynicism and exhaustion we carry, there is a truth still glowing:

You were never meant to burn alone.

Look around.
At the father folding laundry at midnight while his children sleep in another man's country.
At the mother who carries too many jobs and not enough time and still remembers to pack a note in a lunchbox.
At the protester, the healer, the doubter, the one who is quietly trying to forgive a thing they were never meant to endure.

These are not different kinds of people.
These are your people.
This is your family.

The divisions we see are real, yes. They cut and scar and steal.
But they are not final.
They are not the end of our story.

What if the beginning of our healing isn't found in argument or conquest, but in reverence?
What if we approached each other not as strangers or threats, but as siblings separated by grief?

We all want the same things.
To feel safe.
To be seen.
To be held.
To know that our life means something beyond the small boxes we check or the papers we sign.

And when we are brave enough to see that same longing in one another, when we recognize the divine spark behind someone's tired eyes or broken story, we begin to rebuild the world, one sacred connection at a time.

The Flame and the Human Family

The story of us is not finished.
It's unfolding, flame by flame, soul by soul, hand by hand.

We do not need to agree on everything.

We don't need to worship the same way, or dress the same way, or speak the same tongue.
But we do need to remember that we are a family.
Imperfect. Fragile. Fierce. Sacred.

The question is not, "What do we do with our differences?"

The real question is,
"How do we love anyway?"

Let this be the first page of your remembering.
Let this be the light you carry forward.
Let this be the story we begin again together.

Chapter Two: What Divides Us, What Unites Us

We were not born afraid of each other.
No child looks at another and sees a threat.
They see another set of eyes, a hand to grab, a voice to mimic, a laugh to share.
Division is not our nature. It's something we're taught.

Sometimes it's taught in whispers.
Don't trust them.
They're not like us.
Stay close to your kind.

Sometimes it's taught in systems, the kind we don't question because they're older than our parents and dressed up in laws and policies and flags.
And sometimes it's not taught at all, it's inherited. Breathed in.
Absorbed through pain we didn't cause but now carry.

What divides us is rarely the thing we argue about on the surface.
It's not really politics, or geography, or even faith.

The Flame and the Human Family

It's the wounds underneath.

Wounds of being left out.
Of being told we're less than.
Of being silenced, ignored, labeled, blamed.
Of being told that our story doesn't matter, or worse, doesn't exist.

And so we form tribes.
Not the sacred kind, but the defensive kind,
the kind built from pain, held together by suspicion, and armed
with stories we tell ourselves to survive.

But here's the truth that waits underneath all of it:
Most people are not trying to be right.
They're trying to be safe.

They raise their voice not to dominate, but because they are afraid
of not being heard.
They cling to identity not because they hate yours, but because they
don't know who they are without it.

We are all, in our own way, trying to come home.

The Flame and the Human Family

What unites us is quieter than what divides us, which is why it's easy to miss.
It doesn't shout.
It hums.

It hums in the mother wiping her child's face with the corner of her shirt.
In the old man who still wears his wedding ring decades after she's gone.
In the teenager staring out a window wondering if he matters.
In the nurse holding a stranger's hand at 3:00 AM because no one else came.

It hums in the deepest parts of us, the part that longs to be known without having to explain ourselves.

The same sun rises over temples and mosques and cathedrals.
The same rain falls on the joyful and the grieving.
The same breath fills our lungs, no matter what flag hangs above us.

Our differences are real.
But so is our sameness.

The Flame and the Human Family

We all bury our dead.
We all laugh when children dance.
We all need someone to sit beside us when the world caves in.

The great tragedy is not that we are different.
It's that we've been convinced our differences must mean division.
But the world was never meant to be flat and monochrome.

It was meant to be a mosaic, a communion of contrast.
Not uniformity, but unity.

So what do we do with what divides us?

We acknowledge it.
We name it.
We grieve it.

Then we walk through it, not around it, until we find one another again.

Because the truth is, every time we choose connection over comfort,
every time we let empathy interrupt our certainty,
every time we remember that the person in front of us has cried in

the dark just like we have.

We build a longer table.

And that is how the world begins again.

This is what unites us:

Not perfect agreement.

Not sameness.

But shared humanity, and the courage to keep loving through the differences.

Chapter Three: Race, Roots, and the Rainbow of Creation

We were never meant to look the same.

The first brushstrokes of humanity were laid not in black and white, but in ochres and coppers, deep browns and golden tones kissed by sun and earth. The Creator did not paint in grayscale, the garden was full of color, and so were we.

We were not made different by mistake.
We were made different by design.

And yet, for so long, difference became the dividing line.
Not a marvel, but a measure.
Not a gift, but a judgment.

Somewhere along the line, someone decided that to be white was to be closer to heaven, and to be black or brown or something in between was to be further from the light. That was not God's decree. That was man's fear, built into systems and schools and skin.

The Flame and the Human Family

It started as whispers.

Then it became rulebooks, borders, bloodlines.

Then it became chains.

And still, somehow, we survived.

We sang in the fields.

We carved wisdom into wood and scar.

We braided memory into hair.

We carried the ancestors in our rhythm, even when the world tried to erase the beat.

This chapter is not about guilt.

It's not about blame.

It's about truth.

And the truth is this: race has been misused.

Weaponized. Twisted into a hierarchy it was never meant to be.

But that's not the end of the story.

Because underneath the bruises of empire and the silences of erased history, there is something eternal that remains: the sacredness of difference.

Your skin is not a mistake.

The Flame and the Human Family

Your hair is not a problem.
Your language, your lineage, your rituals, they are threads in a divine tapestry that is still being woven.

When we talk about race, we are not just talking about politics.
We're talking about story.
About roots.
About how we see ourselves, and how we allow others to see us.

And when those stories are distorted, made to seem lesser, or exotic, or threatening, we forget that all of us came from the same beginning:
A people made of earth and breath.
A people formed in the image of the divine.

You want to know something sacred?

Africa is not poor.
It is plundered.
Indigenous is not primitive.
It is protective.
Brown is not broken.
It is born of sunlight and strength.

And white, white is not the enemy.

The Flame and the Human Family

It is a color in the rainbow. It belongs too, when it remembers it is part of the circle, not above it.

There is no healing in pretending we are all the same.
There is healing in honoring that we are not, and loving anyway.

Your color is not your cage.
It is your calling.
To show what God looks like through your lens.
To carry forward the wisdom of your people.
To sit in the circle without having to shrink, and without needing to dominate.

We were made different not to compete,
But to complete the picture.

If you believe in a God who paints the sky with color,
Then believe also in a God who made you radiant on purpose.

If you believe in the Body of humanity,
Then understand: we are not meant to be a single limb or tone or rhythm.
We are meant to be a symphony.

Race is not what divides us.

The Flame and the Human Family

The lie about race is.

And now, now is the time to remember.
Let the rainbow rise.
Let every culture shine.
Let us walk back into the garden, not to become the same,
But to see how beautiful we've always been together.

Part II: The Flame Within

Inside every human heart is a spark of the divine. Some call it spirit, others call it soul, but we call it the flame. This is not the property of one people or one religion it is a gift to all. We explore how that flame connects us, and how we can protect it in ourselves and others.

The Flame and the Human Family

The Flame and the Human Family

Chapter Four: Every Soul Has a Spark

Somewhere along the way, someone told you that your worth was conditional.

Maybe they didn't say it outright, maybe they didn't have to.
Maybe it came through a look.
A silence.
A door that never opened.
A spotlight that never turned your way.

But you felt it.
The shrinking.
The second-guessing.
The ache of being overlooked, even when you were trying your best to shine.

Let me tell you something they forgot to mention:

Your light was never up for debate.
It doesn't depend on success.

The Flame and the Human Family

It doesn't vanish because of failure.
It doesn't shrink because the world didn't clap when you walked in the room.

It is your birthright.
It came with you.
And it burns, even when you can't feel the heat.

Every soul has a spark.
It's not a metaphor. It's not spiritual fluff.
It's real.
A divine ember inside your being, glowing, steady, quiet, waiting to be remembered.

Not everyone feels theirs all the time.
That doesn't mean it's gone.
It means life has covered it in ash.
The kind of ash that builds from grief.
From rejection.
From silence.
From trying to be something you're not for too long.

But no matter how covered, how buried, how forgotten,

The Flame and the Human Family

the spark does not die.

It waits.
For a breath.

For a moment of stillness.
For someone to remind you that you matter.

This is that reminder.

You are not empty.
You are not behind.
You are not late.
You are not broken.
You are carrying fire, and it is still yours.

The world we live in doesn't make it easy to believe that.
It's loud, fast, demanding.
It asks you to prove your value with numbers, performance, productivity.
It tells you that you are only as good as what you produce, or how well you fit in.

But your spark didn't come from the world.

The Flame and the Human Family

So, the world doesn't get to define it.

It came from something older, deeper, holy.
It came from the same breath that lit the stars.

Think of all the people who lit your path, and didn't even know it.

The teacher who listened.
The stranger who smiled.
The ancestor who prayed before your name was ever spoken.
The quiet one who didn't say much, but whose presence made the room feel safer.

Not all flames are loud.
Some are steady.
Some are hidden.
Some are so deep they only show when someone else is in the dark.

Don't underestimate your light because it doesn't look like someone else's.
The spark is yours.
And the way you carry it is sacred.

You don't have to become someone else to be radiant.
You don't have to fix everything to be worthy.

The Flame and the Human Family

You just have to keep the flame alive, and trust that it was never small to begin with.

If you're tired, let this be your rest.
If you're doubting, let this be your truth.
If you've forgotten who you are,
remember this:

Your soul carries the light of God.
Your story is a lantern.
And someone else is walking their way home by it.

Let it burn.
Let it warm you.
Let it remind the world what is possible when one person dares to stay lit.

Chapter 5: Faith Beyond the Fence

There comes a moment in many lives when the structure we inherited no longer holds the fullness of our spirit. The pews that once offered us peace feel too small for the questions we've grown into. The verses we memorized begin to ache for deeper meaning. This is the moment we begin to look beyond the fence.

Faith, when rooted in fear, becomes a prison. But faith, when rooted in love, becomes a bridge. A bridge that reaches beyond labels and boundaries, beyond denominations and divisions. A bridge to something not smaller, but infinitely greater.

I was raised in a church where hymns echoed through stained glass windows and robes swept the floor with ritual. I do not regret those days. They gave me discipline, gave me form, gave me the holy hunger. But the table felt set for a few, not all. And God, as I came to know Him, was too big for that room.

There is a fence around every doctrine that says, "Only we have the truth." But the Divine cannot be domesticated. You can no more own God than you can bottle a sunrise. To believe otherwise is to commit spiritual theft.

In this chapter, we do not call for a demolition of churches or temples. We call for open doors, open hearts, open altars. We call for a restoration of the original fire, not the institution, but the encounter.

For those who have felt cast out, who were told they did not fit the mold, your faith is valid. Your journey is sacred. Your questions are welcome. You are not backsliding; you are expanding.

Let your faith be wide enough to hold wonder. Deep enough to cradle doubt. Brave enough to evolve. The Flame of One is not a rejection of God, it is a return to God, without the fences that divide His children.

In the days ahead, the world will not need more churches built with bricks. It will need living temples, humans who carry the holy into every space they enter.

Let your life be that temple. Let your soul be the scripture someone else reads. Let your kindness be the sermon that heals.

Faith beyond the fence is not faith without roots, it is faith with wings.

Chapter 6: Healing from Religion, Returning to God

For many, religion has been a place of comfort and meaning. For others, it has been a source of pain, exclusion, and disillusionment. In this chapter, we acknowledge both truths. We confront the shadows cast by religious institutions while affirming the enduring light of the Divine that no system can contain or extinguish.

We live in a world where more people than ever are leaving organized religion. Some leave quietly, others leave wounded. They carry stories of rejection for asking questions, for loving differently, for being born into bodies or identities that were not deemed "acceptable." Others leave because they are tired of performance, of pretending, of chasing grace through fear.

But walking away from religion does not mean walking away from God.

If anything, for many, it is the first step back.

The Wound and the Wonder

There is a wound that only some will understand: the ache of longing for the sacred after being told you don't belong in sacred spaces. But there is also a wonder that only the free can taste: the rediscovery of God outside the walls of dogma.

Many who have been hurt by religion still hunger for connection, transcendence, and meaning. They still pray. Still hope. Still seek.

Here in The Flame of One, we honor those stories. We see the faith behind the fear, the spark beneath the ashes. We are not here to erase the past, but to kindle a new fire. One that does not burn with judgment, but with welcome. One that warms the cold places where people were once made to feel less than holy.

Returning, Not Rejecting

To return to God is not to reject all religion, nor to shame those who find life within it. It is to return to the Source. The heart. The One.

It is to remember that God was never confined to temples, doctrines, or creeds. God is spirit and truth. Breath and being. Closer than our next thought. Larger than our deepest question.

The Flame and the Human Family

We are not alone. We are not forsaken. And we were never outside the reach of love.

Kindling New Altars

Some of us still light candles. Some still kneel. Some meditate in silence. Some sing in circles. The form may change, but the flame remains. Each act of love, justice, courage, or compassion is its own kind of prayer.

To heal from religion is not to discard it all. It is to sift what is sacred from what was harmful. To rebuild what was broken. To reclaim what was always ours.

The sacred is not scarce. It is abundant. And it is calling us home.

Reflection Questions:

- What has been your experience with religion, and how has it shaped your spiritual path?
- In what ways have you encountered God beyond religion?
- What would it look like to create a spiritual practice that feels true and life-giving to you today?

Blessing: May the wounds inflicted in the name of God be healed by the presence of God. May you walk in the truth that you are already holy. And may every step forward be a return to the flame within.

Part III: Wounded World, Sacred Path

We live in a world marked by fracture and fear, a planet aching for healing, a people searching for purpose. But even in the shadows, the sacred path still calls. In this final section, we explore how to walk with compassion through a divided world, how to let our wounds become wisdom, and how to answer the call of love with courage, community, and action. This is where the flame becomes movement not just within, but beyond.

Chapter 7: The Age of Fear and the Call of Love

We live in a time marked not only by unprecedented change but by an undercurrent of anxiety that flows through every part of our world. Fear is in the air we breathe, the news we watch, the algorithms we scroll. But beneath this storm, there is a whisper that refuses to be silenced: the call of love.

The age of fear is not just about war or economic collapse. It is also about the erosion of trust. In leaders. In systems. In each other. We find ourselves shrinking, retreating into tribalism, building walls instead of bridges. Even faith communities, which should be sanctuaries, are not always immune. And yet, there is another path.

The World on Edge

When we look around, we see a world aching under the weight of division. Politicians pit neighbor against neighbor. Social media rewards outrage. Entire generations grow up with more connection but less community. Anxiety, depression, and isolation are the silent epidemics of our time.

But it is not new.

History shows us cycles of fear. From the crusades to colonization, from slavery to segregation, fear has often worn the mask of righteousness. But every time fear tries to reign, there are those who answer with something stronger: love.

Love is not weakness. Love is not blind. Love is not passive.

It is the most radical resistance of all.

The Call of Love

The call of love is not a romantic notion; it is a spiritual revolution. It asks us to stay open when we want to close. To listen when we want to shout. To reach when we want to retreat.

Love calls us to create communities that heal instead of harm. Homes that nurture instead of judge. Movements that honor every soul instead of requiring sameness.

The Flame of One is that kind of movement.

We are not here to escape the world, but to light it up.

The Flame and the Human Family

We gather in a circle, not a hierarchy.
We move through music, not marching orders.
We lead with welcome, not with warnings.

And we begin with love.

Courage in the Fire

To answer the call of love in the age of fear takes courage. It is a quiet, persistent courage. The courage to be kind in a cruel world. The courage to keep your heart open. The courage to believe in the sacredness of humanity, even when history says otherwise.

You may not always feel brave. You may not always feel hopeful. But still, you can answer the call.

Light a candle.
Speak a truth.
Hold someone's hand.
Refuse to hate.

This is how the world changes.

The Flame and the Human Family

Reflection Questions:

- Where do you see fear showing up in your own life or community?

- What practices help you stay grounded in love?

- How can you be a presence of peace in a frightened world?

Blessing:

May fear lose its grip on your heart.

May love be your first language.

And may your life become a lantern that leads others home.

Chapter 8: Stories from the Firelight

Testimonies, Parables, and Soul Lessons from the Human Family

There is something ancient and sacred about gathering around a fire.

It is where ancestors told their stories, where wisdom was passed down without pages, where healing began through shared words and knowing silences. Around the fire, no one is greater. No one is forgotten. Every voice is honored. Every story is a spark.

This chapter is our firelight, a place to gather the real and raw experiences of being human. Each testimony and parable you find here is a flame that once flickered in darkness and still burns to warm another soul.

1. The Man with the Empty Bowl

There was a man who walked from village to village with nothing but a bowl in his hand. People thought he was mad. "Why do you carry an empty bowl?" they asked.

"I carry it to remind me of how full I used to think I was."

He had once been rich, praised, honored. But life had emptied him. Loss, betrayal, sickness, he lost everything that once filled his identity.

Yet he smiled more now.

One day, a child came to him and asked, "Are you hungry?"

He looked down at the bowl, then at the child. "I am not empty to be filled with food," he said, "but to be filled with what lasts."

The child placed a flower in the bowl.

The man wept.

Reflection:

Sometimes it is our emptiness that prepares us to receive the truth. What have you lost that made space for something deeper?

2. The Woman Who Forgave the Ocean

In a small coastal village, there was a woman whose husband had been taken by the sea. A storm swallowed his boat. No body was found.

For years, she cursed the ocean. She would not go near it. She would not speak its name.

One morning, an orphaned child wandered too close to the waves and nearly drowned. Without thinking, the woman ran to save her, diving into the water.

When they emerged, breathless, she held the child and realized: the sea that had taken also gave.

"I had been speaking to the sea as a thief," she said, "but today it spoke to me as a mother."

She went on to teach ocean safety, bless the tides, and tell her story by the shore. Her grief did not vanish. But it began to flow again.

Reflection:

What grief are you holding that might one day become a gift to others? Can healing and hurt coexist?

3. *Elijah's Ashes*

Elijah was a boy who always felt invisible. At school, at home, even in church, no one really saw him.

One day he found an old fireplace in the woods behind his grandmother's house. It hadn't been used in years. Elijah gathered dry sticks, struck stones together, and made a small flame.

He went back every day to tend it.

He began to talk to it.

The fire listened.

It did not correct his feelings. It did not ask him to be different. It simply warmed his words.

Years later, Elijah became a social worker. He created community spaces where young people could talk and be heard.

Each center had a small fireplace, not because it was cold, but because it was sacred.

"I wasn't healed by answers," he said. "I was healed by being allowed to speak my pain without interruption."

Reflection:

Do you remember a moment when you felt truly seen or heard? How might you offer that gift to someone else?

4. The Candle and the Mirror

There once was a candle that burned brightly in a quiet temple. It lit the room night after night without complaint.

One day, a mirror was placed beside it. The candle looked into the mirror and for the first time saw itself burning.

It was startled and humbled.

"I did not know I gave so much light," it said.

The mirror replied, "You have no idea how many have been guided by your flame. You burn, and they find their way."

Reflection:

Who has been a candle in your life? Who reflects your light when you forget it? Could you be the mirror for someone else?

5. The Circle That Never Closed

A man once drew a circle in the sand and said, "Only the righteous may enter here."

So, people stepped away, unsure of their worth.

But another man came and drew a wider circle that included everyone standing near and those who had stepped away. He said, "This is the circle of belonging."

Someone asked, "But what about justice?"

And he said, "Justice is not destroyed by inclusion. It is fulfilled by love."

Reflection:

How do we draw our circles? With chalk or chains? With fear or faith? With the openness of love or the caution of judgment?

Final Blessing Around the Fire

May these stories remind you that your wounds have wisdom, your losses have lessons, and your light, however small, matters.

This is not the end of the firelight, it is an invitation.

Come. Share your story. Add your spark. There is room for you here.

Chapter 9: The Way of the Flame (practices, community, call to action)

There comes a moment on every spiritual journey when insight asks for embodiment. When awakening asks not only to be felt, but to be lived. That moment is now.

We have told the story of our humanity. We have traced our wounds and honored our roots. We have reclaimed the divine spark that lives in each of us. But now we turn to the path forward.

We call this path **The Way of the Flame**.

It is not a religion, nor a rigid set of rules. It is a living way, shaped by compassion, ignited by community, guided by grace.

It is not something you must believe. It is something you can practice.

1. Walk as Flame-Bearers

To walk the Way of the Flame is to see yourself and others as bearers of sacred fire. Every soul you meet holds a light. Some

The Flame and the Human Family

bright. Some flickering. Some nearly extinguished by the winds of life.

Our task is not to judge the flame, but to protect it.

We move through the world like lanterns: steady, kind, radiant.

Whether in joy or in sorrow, we carry the light.

2. Gather in Circles, Not Pyramids

Hierarchy builds towers. Love builds circles.

In our gatherings, whether two people or two hundred we strive for spiritual equality. We listen as much as we speak. We honor the wisdom in every voice. We let tears be teachers and silence be sacred.

The Flame of One is a circle of belonging, not a pulpit of control. We walk together, not above one another.

3. Practice the Flame

A flame must be tended, or it goes out.

The Way of the Flame invites you to build your own spiritual rhythm a daily or weekly practice that nurtures your inner fire.

Some suggestions:

- Morning stillness (5 minutes of breath and gratitude)
- Evening candle prayer (naming your joys and burdens)
- Weekly act of kindness
- Monthly community reflection circle
- Reading sacred writings from different traditions
- Listening deeply to others' stories

These are not mandates. They are invitations. Let the spark guide you.

4. Build a Better World

A flame is not just beautiful. It is powerful. Transformative.

The Way of the Flame is a call to action, to bring light where there is darkness. That means standing for justice. Feeding the hungry. Healing the hurting. Lifting the unheard.

This is not a feel-good movement. It is a love-that-does movement.

Our faith is not private it is communal.

To follow the Way is to ask, **"Where is the pain, and how can I help carry the light?"**

5. Keep the Flame Alive

There will be days when you feel dim. When doubt visits. When exhaustion robs you of wonder.

On those days, let the community carry you. Let someone else's flame light yours. And when you're strong again, you'll light another's.

The Way of the Flame is not walked alone.

We tend this fire together.

Epilogue

"The Fire We Carry Forward"

We have walked a long road together.

From the first page, you've been invited not only to read, but to remember.
To remember who you are. Who *we* are. And the fire that flickers quietly or fiercely within us all.

This book has never been about building a new religion.
It's about *returning* to the sacred truth that was always ours:
That we are one human family. Diverse, divine, and drenched in possibility.

We've spoken of race, and roots. Of wounds and walls. Of spirit and soul.
But beyond the words is something else, something holy:
A call.

A call not to separate, but to **see**.
Not to fight one another, but to **fight for one another**.
Not to burn bridges, but to **be the firelight that welcomes the weary home**.

The Flame and the Human Family

We are not naïve.

The world is trembling.

People are divided, disillusioned, afraid.

But so were the prophets. So were the healers. So were the midwives of every great movement.

And so are you.

You were born for a time like this, not to be perfect, but to be **present**.

Not to shout louder, but to **listen deeper**.

Not to carry torches of rage, but to **tend flames of grace**.

This book ends.

But the flame continues.

Carry it with you.

Fan it in others.

Let it be the warmth in cold spaces, the light in dark places, and the reminder always

that no matter how different we look, love, speak, or struggle,

We belong to one another.

And that is sacred ground.

The Flame and the Human Family

Letter to the Flamebearers

Dear Keeper of the Flame,

If you've read this far, then this movement is already alive in you.

You may not have a pulpit. You may not wear a title.
But if your heart stirred even once while reading these pages, then you are already a bearer of light.

The Flame of One does not belong to me. It belongs to us, to every soul who chooses love over fear, presence over performance, and justice over comfort.

You are not too late. You are not too small.
You are right on time.

Let your home become a hearth.
Let your work become a witness.
Let your life become a lantern.

Wherever you are, begin there.
With a gesture.
A gathering.
A remembering.

The Flame and the Human Family

Light a candle.

Speak a word.

Make room for someone who never thought they belonged.

And if you ever wonder whether this light can truly change the world, remember:

It already has.

It's changing you.

And that is how the fire spreads.

With hope and holy fire,

Dean Nkulumo Maphenduka
Umlindi WeLangabi Elingcwele
Guardian of the Sacred Flame

The Flame and the Human Family

Blessing

"For the Carriers of Light"

May you walk lightly, but never doubt the weight of your worth.
May your heart stay soft in a world growing numb.
May you make space for joy without apology, and for grief without shame.

May your ancestors speak peace to your spirit.
And may your descendants inherit a better world because you were here.

When you are tired, may rest find you.
When you are bold, may justice follow.
When you are afraid, may love anchor you.

And when you feel like you've lost the flame,
may you remember that even a single ember can still start a revolution of hope.

Go now, not in silence, but in stillness.

Not in haste, but in holy purpose.

And may the Flame of One go before you, within you, and through you

until all the world is warmed by the truth:

We are one family.

The Flame and the Human Family

A Prayer for the World

"In This Fragile Hour"

O Eternal Flame,
God of every tongue and no tongue,
Mother-Father Spirit of sky, soil, and soul.

We cry to You from a world unraveling.

Our streets echo with sorrow.
Our nations tremble with division.
Our children inherit anxiety instead of dreams.
Our elders carry wisdom few pause to hear.

And still, You are here.
In breath.
In fire.
In us.

Remind us what it means to be human
to be humble, to be holy, to be home to one another.

Teach us again to listen without fear,
to speak without harm,
to love without condition.

The Flame and the Human Family

Break down the lies we've built into systems.
Heal what hate has hardened.
Unmake the myth of supremacy.
Uncoil the roots of cruelty.
Undo every altar that requires someone's exclusion for another's inclusion.

Let compassion rise in boardrooms and kitchens,
in courtrooms and congregations,
in the hearts of presidents and the hands of neighbors.

Let us trade despair for daring.
Noise for nuance.
Walls for welcome.

And let no one no child, no elder, no refugee, no enemy
be outside the reach of Your grace.

May the next war never be needed.
May the next healing come sooner.
May we not wait for permission to do what is just,
or delay what we know is right.

May we remember:
We are not many tribes fighting for scraps.
We are one family learning how to forgive.

Amen.

The Flame and the Human Family

Let it be so.

Let it begin in me.

Let it begin in us.

Let it begin now.